NONES

NONES

W. H. AUDEN

RANDOM HOUSE · NEW YORK

Fourth Printing

ACKNOWLEDGMENT IS HERE MADE TO THE FOLLOWING MAGAZINES IN WHICH SOME OF THE POEMS OF THIS VOLUME FIRST APPEARED: *The American Scholar, Atlantic Monthly, Harper's Magazine, The Harvard Advocate, Commentary, Horizon, The Kenyon Review, Ladies' Home Journal, The Listener, Mademoiselle, The Nation, The New Yorker, The Reporter, Poetry* (London), *The Third Hour* and *This Changing World*.

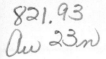
To Reinhold and Ursula Niebuhr

We, too, had known golden hours
When body and soul were in tune,
Had danced with our true loves
By the light of a full moon
And sat with the wise and good
As tongues grew witty and gay
Over some noble dish
Out of Escoffier;
Had felt the intrusive glory
Which tears reserve apart
And would in the old grand manner
Have sung from a resonant heart.
But, pawed-at and gossipped-over
By the promiscuous crowd,
Concocted by editors
Into spells to befuddle the crowd,
All words like peace and love,
All sane affirmative speech,
Had been soiled, profaned, debased
To a horrid mechanical screech:
No civil style survived
That pandaemonium
But the wry, the sotto-voce,
Ironic and monochrome:
And where should we find shelter
For joy or mere content
When little was left standing
But the suburb of dissent.

Contents

Prime

Simultaneously, as soundlessly,
    Spontaneously, suddenly
As, at the vaunt of the dawn, the kind
    Gates of the body fly open
To its world beyond, the gates of the mind,
    The horn gate and the ivory gate
Swing to, swing shut, instantaneously
    Quell the nocturnal rummage
Of its rebellious fronde, ill-favored,
    Ill-natured and second-rate,
Disenfranchised, widowed and orphaned
    By an historical mistake:
Recalled from the shades to be a seeing being,
    From absence to be on display,
Without a name or history I wake
    Between my body and the day.

Holy this moment, wholly in the right,
    As, in complete obedience
To the light's laconic outcry, next
    As a sheet, near as a wall,
Out there as a mountain's poise of stone,
    The world is present, about,
And I know that I am, here, not alone
    But with a world, and rejoice
Unvexed, for the will has still to claim
    This adjacent arm as my own.
The memory to name me, resume
    Its routine of praise and blame,
And smiling to me is this instant while

Still the day is intact and I
The Adam sinless in our beginning,
    Adam still previous to any act.

I draw breath; that is of course to wish
    No matter what to be wise
To be different to die and the cost
    No matter how is Paradise
Lost of course and myself owing a death:
    The eager ridge, the steady sea,
The flat roofs of the fishing village
    Still asleep in its bunny,
Though as fresh and sunny still are not friends
    But things to hand, this ready flesh
No honest equal but my accomplice now
    My assassin to be and my name
Stands for my historical share of care
    For a lying self-made city,
Afraid of our living task, the dying
    Which the coming day will ask.

In Praise of Limestone

If it form the one landscape that we the inconstant ones
    Are consistently homesick for, this is chiefly
Because it dissolves in water. Mark these rounded slopes
    With their surface fragrance of thyme and beneath
A secret system of caves and conduits; hear these springs
    That spurt out everywhere with a chuckle
Each filling a private pool for its fish and carving
    Its own little ravine whose cliffs entertain
The butterfly and the lizard; examine this region
    Of short distances and definite places:
What could be more like Mother or a fitter background
    For her son, for the nude young male who lounges
Against a rock displaying his dildo, never doubting
    That for all his faults he is loved, whose works are but
Extensions of his power to charm? From weathered outcrop
    To hill-top temple, from appearing waters to
Conspicuous fountains, from a wild to a formal vineyard,
    Are ingenious but short steps that a child's wish
To receive more attention than his brothers, whether
    By pleasing or teasing, can easily take.

Watch, then, the band of rivals as they climb up and down
    Their steep stone gennels in twos and threes, sometimes
Arm in arm, but never, thank God, in step; or engaged
    On the shady side of a square at midday in
Voluble discourse, knowing each other too well to think
    There are any important secrets, unable
To conceive a god whose temper-tantrums are moral
    And not to be pacified by a clever line

Or a good lay: for, accustomed to a stone that responds,
    They have never had to veil their faces in awe
Of a crater whose blazing fury could not be fixed;
    Adjusted to the local needs of valleys
Where everything can be touched or reached by walking,
    Their eyes have never looked into infinite space
Through the lattice-work of a nomad's comb; born lucky,
    Their legs have never encountered the fungi
And insects of the jungle, the monstrous forms and lives
    With which we have nothing, we like to hope, in common.
So, when one of them goes to the bad, the way his mind works
    Remains comprehensible: to become a pimp
Or deal in fake jewelry or ruin a fine tenor voice
    For effects that bring down the house could happen to all
But the best and the worst of us . . .
                                    That is why, I suppose,
    The best and worst never stayed here long but sought
Immoderate soils where the beauty was not so external,
    The light less public and the meaning of life
Something more than a mad camp. "Come!" cried the granite wastes,
    "How evasive is your humor, how accidental
Your kindest kiss, how permanent is death." (Saints-to-be
    Slipped away sighing.) "Come!" purred the clays and gravels.
"On our plains there is room for armies to drill; rivers
    Wait to be tamed and slaves to construct you a tomb
In the grand manner: soft as the earth is mankind and both
    Need to be altered." (Intendant Caesars rose and
Left, slamming the door.) But the really reckless were fetched
    By an older colder voice, the oceanic whisper:
"I am the solitude that asks and promises nothing;

14

That is how I shall set you free. There is no love;
There are only the various envies, all of them sad."

They were right, my dear, all those voices were right
And still are; this land is not the sweet home that it looks,
    Nor its peace the historical calm of a site
Where something was settled once and for all: A backward
    And delapidated province, connected
To the big busy world by a tunnel, with a certain
    Seedy appeal, is that all it is now? Not quite:
It has a worldly duty which in spite of itself
    It does not neglect, but calls into question
All the Great Powers assume; it disturbs our rights. The poet,
    Admired for his earnest habit of calling
The sun the sun, his mind Puzzle, is made uneasy
    By these solid statues which so obviously doubt
His antimythological myth; and these gamins,
    Pursuing the scientist down the tiled colonnade
With such lively offers, rebuke his concern for Nature's
    Remotest aspects: I, too, am reproached, for what
And how much you know. Not to lose time, not to get caught,
    Not to be left behind, not, please! to resemble
The beasts who repeat themselves, or a thing like water
    Or stone whose conduct can be predicted, these
Are our Common Prayer, whose greatest comfort is music
    Which can be made anywhere, is invisible,
And does not smell. In so far as we have to look forward
    To death as a fact, not doubt we are right: But if
Sins can be forgiven, if bodies rise from the dead,
    These modifications of matter into

Innocent athletes and gesticulating fountains,
    Made solely for pleasure, make a further point:
The blessed will not care what angle they are regarded from,
    Having nothing to hide. Dear, I know nothing of
Either, but when I try to imagine a faultless love
    Or the life to come, what I hear is the murmur
Of underground streams, what I see is a limestone landscape.

One Circumlocution

Sometimes we see astonishingly clearly
The out-there-when we are already in;
Now that is not what we are here-for really.

All its to-do is bound to re-occur,
Is nothing therefore that we need to say;
How then to make its compromise refer

To what could not be otherwise instead
And has its being as its own to be,
The once-for-all that is not seen nor said?

Tell for the power how to thunderclaps
The graves flew open, the rivers ran up-hill;
Such staged importance is at most perhaps.

Speak well of moonlight on a winding stair,
Of light-boned children under great green oaks;
The wonder, yes, but death should not be there.

One circumlocution as used as any
Depends, it seems, upon the joke of rhyme
For the pure joy; else why should so many

Poems which make us cry direct us to
Ourselves at our least apt, least kind, least true,
Where a blank I loves blankly a blank You?

Their Lonely Betters

As I listened from a beach-chair in the shade
To all the noises that my garden made,
It seemed to me only proper that words
Should be withheld from vegetables and birds.

A robin with no Christian name ran through
The Robin-Anthem which was all it knew,
And rustling flowers for some third party waited
To say which pairs, if any, should get mated.

No one of them was capable of lying,
There was not one which knew that it was dying
Or could have with a rhythm or a rhyme
Assumed responsibility for time.

Let them leave language to their lonely betters
Who count some days and long for certain letters;
We, too, make noises when we laugh or weep,
Words are for those with promises to keep.

Serenade

On and on and on
The forthright catadoup
Shouts at the stone-deaf stone;
Over and over again,
Singly or as a group,
Weak diplomatic men
With a small defiant light
Salute the incumbent night.

With or without a mind,
Chafant or outwardly calm,
Each thing has an axe to grind
And exclaims its matter-of-fact;
The child with careful charm
Or a sudden opprobrious act,
The tiger, the griping fern,
Extort the world's concern.

All, all, have rights to declare,
Not one is man enough
To be, simply, publicly, there
With no private emphasis;
So my embodied love
Which, like most feeling, is
Half humbug and half true,
Asks neighborhood of you.

Song

Deftly, admiral, cast your fly
    Into the slow deep hover,
Till the wise old trout mistake and die;
    Salt are the deeps that cover
    The glittering fleets you led,
      White is your head.

Read on, ambassador, engrossed
    In your favourite Stendhal;
The Outer Provinces are lost,
    Unshaven horsemen swill
    The great wines of the Châteaux
      Where you danced long ago.

Do not turn, do not lift, your eyes
    Toward the still pair standing
On the bridge between your properties,
    Indifferent to your minding:
    In its glory, in its power,
      This is their hour.

Nothing your strength, your skill, could do
    Can alter their embrace
Or dispersuade the Furies who
    At the appointed place
    With claw and dreadful brow
      Wait for them now.

The Love Feast

In an upper room at midnight
See us gathered on behalf
Of love according to the gospel
Of the radio-phonograph.

Lou is telling Anne what Molly
Said to Mark behind her back;
Jack likes Jill who worships George
Who has the hots for Jack.

Catechumens make their entrance;
Steep enthusiastic eyes
Flicker after tits and baskets;
Someone vomits; someone cries.

Willy cannot bear his father,
Lilian is afraid of kids;
The Love that rules the sun and stars
Permits what He forbids.

Adrian's pleasure-loving dachshund
In a sinner's lap lies curled;
Drunken absent-minded fingers
Pat a sinless world.

Who is Jenny lying to
By long-distance telephone?
The Love that made her out of nothing
Tells me to go home.

But that Miss Number in the corner
Playing hard to get. . . .
I am sorry I'm not sorry . . .
Make me chaste, Lord, but not yet.

Air Port

Let out where two fears intersect, a point selected
    Jointly by general staffs and engineers,
In a wet land, facing rough oceans, never invaded
    By Caesars or a cartesian doubt, I stand,
Pale, half asleep, inhaling its new fresh air that smells
    So strongly of soil and grass, of toil and gender,
But not for long: a professional friend is at hand
    Who smiling leads us indoors; we follow in file,

Obeying that fond peremptory tone reserved for those
    Nervously sick and children one cannot trust
Who might be tempted by ponds or learn some disgusting
    Trick from a ragamuffin. Through modern panes
I admire a limestone hill I have no permission to climb
    And the pearly clouds of a sunset that seems
Oddly early to me: maybe an ambitious lad stares back,
    Dreaming of elsewhere and our godlike freedom.

Somewhere are places where we have really been, dear spaces
    Of our deeds and faces, scenes we remember
As unchanging because there we changed, where shops have names,
    Dogs bark in the dark at a stranger's footfall
And crops grow ripe and cattle fatten under the kind
    Protection of a godling or goddessling
Whose affection has been assigned them, to heed their needs and
    Plead in heaven the special case of their place.

Somewhere, too, unique for each, his frontier dividing
    Past from future, reached and crossed without warning:
That bridge where an ageing destroyer takes his last salute,

In his rear all rivals fawning, in cages
Or dead, ahead a field of wrath; and that narrow pass where,
    Late from a sullen childhood, a fresh creator
Yields, glowing, to a boyish rapture, wild gothic peaks above him,
    Below, Italian sunshine, Italian flesh.

But here we are nowhere, unrelated to day or our mother
    Earth in love or in hate; our occupation
Leaves no trace on this place or each other who do not
    Meet in its mere enclosure but are exposed
As objects for speculation, aggressive creatures
    On their way to their prey but now quite docile,
Told to wait and controlled by a voice that from time to time calls
    Some class of souls to foregather at the gate.

It calls me again to our plane and soon we are floating above
    A possessed congested surface, a world: down there
Motives and natural processes are stirred by spring
    And wrongs and graves grow greenly; slaves in quarries
Against their wills feel the will to live renewed by the song
    Of a loose bird, a maculate city is spared
Through the prayers of illiterate saints and an ancient
    Feud re-opens with the debacle of a river.

Ischia

[FOR BRIAN HOWARD]

There is a time to admit how much the sword decides,
With flourishing horns to salute the conqueror,
    Impassive, cloaked and great on
    Horseback under his faffling flag.

Changes of heart should also occasion song, like his
Who, turning back from the crusaders' harbor, broke
    With our aggressive habit
    Once and for all and was the first

To see all penniless creatures as his siblings: Then
At all times it is good to praise the shining earth,
    Dear to us whether we choose our
    Duty or do something horrible.

Dearest to each his birthplace; but to recall a green
Valley where mushrooms fatten in the summer nights
    And silvered willows copy
    The circumflexions of the stream

Is not my gladness today: I am presently moved
By sun-drenched Parthenopeia, my thanks are for you,
    Ischia, to whom a fair wind has
    Brought me rejoicing with dear friends

From soiled productive cities. How well you correct
Our injured eyes, how gently you train us to see
    Things and men in perspective
    Underneath your uniform light.

Noble are the plans of the shirt-sleeved engineer,
But luck, you say, does more. What design could have washed
      With such delicate yellows
    And pinks and greens your fishing ports

That lean against ample Epomeo, holding on
To the rigid folds of her skirts? The boiling springs
      Which betray her secret fever
    Make limber the gout-stiffened joint

And improve the venereal act; your ambient peace
In any case is a cure for, ceasing to think
      Of a way to get on, we
    Learn to simply wander about

By twisting paths which at any moment reveal
Some vista as an absolute goal; eastward, perhaps,
      Suddenly there, Vesuvius,
    Looming across the bright bland bay

Like a massive family pudding, or, around
A southern point, sheer-sided Capri who by herself
      Defends the cult of Pleasure,
    A jealous, sometimes a cruel, god.

Always with some cool space or shaded surface, too,
You offer a reason to sit down; tasting what bees
      From the blossoming chestnut
    Or short but shapely dark-haired men

From the aragonian grape distill, your amber wine,
Your coffee-colored honey, we believe that our

Lives are as welcome to us as
Loud explosions are to your saints.

Not that you lie about pain or pretend that a time
Of darkness and outcry will not come back; upon
      Your quays, reminding the happy
   Stranger that all is never well,

Sometimes a donkey breaks out into a choking wail
Of utter protest at what is the case or his
      Master sighs for a Brooklyn
   Where shirts are silk and pants are new,

Far from tall Restituta's all-too-watchful eye,
Whose annual patronage, they say, is bought with blood.
      That, blessed and formidable
   Lady, we hope is not true; but, since

Nothing is free, whatever you charge shall be paid
That these days of exotic splendor may stand out
      In each lifetime like marble
   Mileposts in an alluvial land.

Pleasure Island

What there is as a surround to our figures
    Is very old, very big,
Very formidable indeed; the ocean
    Stares right past us as though
No one here was worth drowning, and the eye, true
    Blue all summer, of the sky
Would not miss a huddle of huts related
    By planks, a dock, a state
Of undress and improvised abandon
    Upon shadowless sand.
To send a cry of protest or a call for
    Protection up into all
Those dazzling miles, to add, however sincerely,
    One's occasional tear
To that volume, would be rather silly,
    Nor is there one small hill
For the hopeful to climb, one tree for the hopeless
    To sit under and mope;
The coast is a blur and without meaning
    The churches and routines
Which stopped there and never cared or dared to
    Cross over to interfere
With this outpost where nothing is wicked
    But to be sorry or sick,
But one thing unneighborly, work. Sometimes
    A visitor may come
With notebooks intending to make its quiet
    Emptiness his ally
In accomplishing immortal chapters,
    But the hasty tap-tap-tap

Of his first day becomes by the second
    A sharp spasmodic peck
And by the third is extinct; we find him
    Next improving his mind
On the beach with a book, but the dozing
    Afternoon is opposed
To rhyme and reason and chamber music,
    The plain sun has no use
For the printing press, the wheel, the electric
    Light, and the waves reject
Sympathy: soon he gives in, stops stopping
    To think, lets his book drop
And lies, like us, on his stomach watching
    As bosom, backside, crotch
Or other sacred trophy is borne in triumph
    Past his adoring by
Souls he does not try to like; then, getting
    Up, gives all to the wet
Clasps of the sea or surrenders his scruples
    To some great gross braying group
That will be drunk till Fall. The tide rises
    And falls, our household ice
Drips to death in the dark and our friendships
    Prepare for a weekend
They will probably not survive: for our
    Lenient amusing shore
Knows in fact about all the dyings, is in
    Fact our place, namely this
Place of a skull, a place where the rose of
    Self-punishment will grow.
The sunset happens, the bar is copious

With fervent life that hopes
To make sense, but down the beach some decaying
    Spirit shambles away,
Kicking idly at driftwood and dead shellfish
    And excusing itself
To itself with evangelical gestures
    For having failed the test:
The moon is up there, but without warning,
    A little before dawn,
Miss Lovely, life and soul of the party,
    Wakes with a dreadful start,
Sure that whatever—O God!—she is in for
    Is about to begin,
Or hearing, beyond the hushabye noises
    Of sea and Me, just a voice
Ask as one might the time or a trifle
    Extra her money and her life.

In Schrafft's

Having finished the Blue-plate Special
And reached the coffee stage,
Stirring her cup she sat,
A somewhat shapeless figure
Of indeterminate age
In an undistinguished hat.

When she lifted her eyes it was plain
That our globular furore,
Our international rout
Of sin and apparatus
And dying men galore,
Was not being bothered about.

Which of the seven heavens
Was responsible her smile
Wouldn't be sure but attested
That, whoever it was, a god
Worth kneeling-to for a while
Had tabernacled and rested.

The Fall of Rome

[FOR CYRIL CONNOLLY]

The piers are pummelled by the waves;
In a lonely field the rain
Lashes an abandoned train;
Outlaws fill the mountain caves.

Fantastic grow the evening gowns;
Agents of the Fisc pursue
Absconding tax-defaulters through
The sewers of provincial towns.

Private rites of magic send
The temple prostitutes to sleep;
All the literati keep
An imaginary friend.

Cerebrotonic Cato may
Extoll the Ancient Disciplines,
But the muscle-bound Marines
Mutiny for food and pay.

Caesar's double-bed is warm
As an unimportant clerk
Writes *I DO NOT LIKE MY WORK*
On a pink official form.

Unendowed with wealth or pity,
Little birds with scarlet legs,
Sitting on their speckled eggs,
Eye each flu-infected city.

Altogether elsewhere, vast
Herds of reindeer move across
Miles and miles of golden moss,
Silently and very fast.

Music Ho

The Emperor's favorite concubine
    Was in the Eunuch's pay,
The Wardens of the Marches turned
    Their spears the other way;
The vases crack, the ladies die,
    The Oracles are wrong:
We suck our thumbs or sleep; the show
    Is gamey and too long.

But—Music Ho!—at last it comes,
    The Transformation Scene:
A rather scruffy-looking god
    Descends in a machine
And, gabbling off his rustic rhymes,
    Misplacing one or two,
Commands the prisoners to walk,
    The enemies to screw.

Nursery Rhyme

Their learned kings bent down to chat with frogs;
This was until the Battle of the Bogs.
The key that opens is the key that rusts.

Their cheerful kings made toffee on their stoves;
This was until the Rotting of the Loaves.
The robins vanish when the ravens come.

That was before the coaches reached the bogs;
Now woolly bears pursue the spotted dogs.
A witch can make an ogre out of mud.

That was before the weevils ate the loaves;
Now blinded bears invade the orange groves.
A witch can make an ogre out of mud.

The woolly bears have polished off the dogs;
Our bowls of milk are full of drowning frogs.
The robins vanish when the ravens come.

The blinded bears have rooted up the groves;
Our poisoned milk boils over on our stoves.
The key that opens is the key that rusts.

The Managers

In the bad old days it was not so bad:
    The top of the ladder
Was an amusing place to sit; success
    Meant quite a lot—leisure
And huge meals, more palaces filled with more
    Objects, books, girls, horses
Than one would ever get round to, and to be
    Carried uphill while seeing
Others walk. To rule was a pleasure when
    One wrote a death-sentence
On the back of the Ace of Spades and played on
    With a new deck. Honours
Are not so physical or jolly now,
    For the species of Powers
We are used to are not like that. Could one of them
    Be said to resemble
The Tragic Hero, the Platonic Saint,
    Or would any painter
Portray one rising triumphant from a lake
    On a dolphin, naked,
Protected by an umbrella of cherubs? Can
    They so much as manage
To behave like genuine Caesars when alone
    Or drinking with cronies,
To let their hair down and be frank about
    The world? It is doubtful.
The last word on how we may live or die
    Rests today with such quiet
Men, working too hard in rooms that are too big,
    Reducing to figures

What is the matter, what is to be done.
 A neat little luncheon
Of sandwiches is brought to each on a tray,
 Nourishment they are able
To take with one hand without looking up
 From papers a couple
Of secretaries are needed to file,
 From problems no smiling
Can dismiss; the typewriters never stop
 But whirr like grasshoppers
In the silent siesta heat as, frivolous
 Across their discussions,
From woods unaltered by our wars and our vows
 There drift the scents of flowers
And the songs of birds who will never vote
 Or bother to notice
Those distinguishing marks a lover sees
 By instinct and policemen
Can be trained to observe; far into the night
 Their windows burn brightly
And, behind their backs bent over some report,
 On every quarter,
For ever like a god or a disease
 There on the earth the reason
In all its aspects why they are tired, the weak,
 The inattentive, seeking
Someone to blame; if, to recuperate
 They go a-playing, their greatness
Encounters the bow of the chef or the glance
 Of the ballet-dancer
Who cannot be ruined by any master's fall.

To rule must be a calling,
It seems, like surgery or sculpture, the fun
 Neither love nor money
But taking necessary risks, the test
 Of one's skill, the question,
If difficult, their own reward. But then
 Perhaps one should mention
Also what must be a comfort as they guess
 In times like the present
When guesses can prove so fatally wrong,
 The fact of belonging
To the very select indeed, to those
 For whom, just supposing
They do, there will be places on the last
 Plane out of disaster.
No; no one is really sorry for their
 Heavy gait and careworn
Look, nor would they thank you if you said you were.

Memorial for the City

*In the self-same point that our soul is made sensual, in the self-same point
is the City of God ordained to him from without beginning.*

Juliana of Norwich

I

The eyes of the crow and the eye of the camera open
Onto Homer's world, not ours. First and last
They magnify earth, the abiding
Mother of gods and men; if they notice either
It is only in passing: gods behave, men die,
Both feel in their own small way, but She
Does nothing and does not care,
She alone is seriously there.

The crow on the crematorium chimney
And the camera roving the battle
Record a space where time has no place.
On the right a village is burning, in a market-town to the left
The soldiers fire, the mayor bursts into tears,
The captives are led away, while far in the distance
A tanker sinks into a dedolant sea.
That is the way things happen; for ever and ever
Plum-blossom falls on the dead, the roar of the waterfall covers
The cries of the whipped and the sighs of the lovers
And the hard bright light composes
A meaningless moment into an eternal fact
Which a whistling messenger disappears with into a defile:
One enjoys glory, one endures shame;
He may, she must. There is no one to blame.

The steady eyes of the crow and the camera's candid eye
See as honestly as they know how, but they lie.
The crime of life is not time. Even now, in this night
Among the ruins of the Post-Vergilian City
Where our past is a chaos of graves and the barbed-wire stretches ahead
Into our future till it is lost to sight,
Our grief is not Greek: As we bury our dead
We know without knowing there is reason for what we bear,
That our hurt is not a desertion, that we are to pity
Neither ourselves nor our city;
Whoever the searchlights catch, whatever the loudspeakers blare,
We are not to despair.

II

Alone in a room Pope Gregory whispered his name
    While the Emperor shone on a centreless world
From wherever he happened to be; the New City rose
    Upon their opposition, the yes and no
Of a rival allegiance; the sword, the local lord
    Were not all; there was home and Rome;
Fear of the stranger was lost on the way to the shrine.

The facts, the acts of the City bore a double meaning:
    Limbs became hymns; embraces expressed in jest
A more permanent tie; infidel faces replaced
    The family foe in the choleric's nightmare;
The children of water parodied in their postures
    The infinite patience of heaven;
Those born under Saturn felt the gloom of the day of doom.

Scribes and innkeepers prospered; suspicious tribes combined
    To rescue Jerusalem from a dull god,

And disciplined logicians fought to recover thought
    From the eccentricities of the private brain
For the Sane City; framed in her windows, orchards, ports,
    Wild beasts, deep rivers and dry rocks
Lay nursed on the smile of a merciful Madonna.

In a sandy province Luther denounced as obscene
    The machine that so smoothly forgave and saved
If paid; he announced to the Sinful City a grinning gap
    No rite could cross; he abased her before the Grace:
Henceforth division was also to be her condition;
    Her conclusions were to include doubt,
Her loves were to bear with her fear; insecure, she endured.

Saints tamed, poets acclaimed the raging herod of the will;
    The groundlings wept as on a secular stage
The grand and the bad went to ruin in thundering verse;
    Sundered by reason and treason the City
Found invisible ground for concord in measured sound,
    While wood and stone learned the shameless
Games of man, to flatter, to show off, be pompous, to romp.

Nature was put to the question in the Prince's name;
    She confessed, what he wished to hear, that she had no soul;
Between his scaffold and her coldness the restrained style,
    The ironic smile became the worldly and devout,
Civility a city grown rich: in his own snob way
    The unarmed gentleman did his job
As a judge to her children, as a father to her forests.

In a national capital Mirabeau and his set
    Attacked mystery; the packed galleries roared

And history marched to the drums of a clear idea,
    The aim of the Rational City, quick to admire,
Quick to tire: she used up Napoleon and threw him away;
    Her pallid affected heroes
Began their hectic quest for the prelapsarian man.

The deserts were dangerous, the waters rough, their clothes
    Absurd but, changing their Beatrices often,
Sleeping little, they pushed on, raised the flag of the Word
    Upon lawless spots denied or forgotten
By the fear or the pride of the Glittering City;
    Guided by hated parental shades,
They invaded and harrowed the hell of her natural self.

Chimeras mauled them, they wasted away with the spleen,
    Suicide picked them off; sunk off Cape Consumption,
Lost on the Tosspot Seas, wrecked on the Gibbering Isles
    Or trapped in the ice of despair at the Soul's Pole,
They died, unfinished, alone; but now the forbidden,
    The hidden, the wild outside were known:
Faithful without faith, they died for the Conscious City.

III

        Across the square,
Between the burnt-out Law Courts and Police Headquarters,
Past the Cathedral far too damaged to repair,
Around the Grand Hotel patched up to hold reporters,
    Near huts of some Emergency Committee,
    The barbed wire runs through the abolished City.

        Across the plains,
Between two hills, two villages, two trees, two friends,

The barbed wire runs which neither argues nor explains
But where it likes a place, a path, a railroad ends,
    The humor, the cuisine, the rites, the taste,
    The pattern of the City, are erased.

    Across our sleep
The barbed wire also runs: It trips us so we fall
And white ships sail without us though the others weep,
It makes our sorry fig-leaf at the Sneerers Ball,
    It ties the smiler to the double bed,
    It keeps on growing from the witch's head.

    Behind the wire
Which is behind the mirror, our Image is the same
Awake or dreaming: It has no image to admire,
No age, no sex, no memory, no creed, no name,
    It can be counted, multiplied, employed
    In any place, at any time destroyed.

    Is it our friend?
No; that is our hope; that we weep and It does not grieve,
That for It the wire and the ruins are not the end:
This is the flesh we are but never would believe,
    The flesh we die but it is death to pity;
    This is Adam waiting for His City.

Let Our Weakness speak

IV

Without me Adam would have fallen irrevocably with Lucifer; he would
    never have been able to cry *O felix culpa.*
It was I who suggested his theft to Prometheus; my frailty cost Adonis
    his life.

I heard Orpheus sing; I was not quite as moved as they say.

I was not taken in by the sheep's-eyes of Narcissus; I was angry with
Psyche when she struck a light.

I was in Hector's confidence; so far as it went.

Had he listened to me Oedipus would never have left Corinth; I
cast no vote at the trial of Orestes.

I fell asleep when Diotima spoke of love; I was not responsible for
the monsters which tempted St. Anthony.

To me the Saviour permitted His Fifth Word from the cross; to be a
stumbling-block to the stoics.

I was the unwelcome third at the meetings of Tristan with Isolda;
they tried to poison me.

I rode with Galahad on his Quest for the San Graal; without under-
standing I kept his vow.

I was the just impediment to the marriage of Faustus with Helen;
I know a ghost when I see one.

With Hamlet I had no patience; but I forgave Don Quixote all for his
admission in the cart.

I was the missing entry in Don Giovanni's list; for which he could
never account.

I assisted Figaro the Barber in all his intrigues; when Prince Tamino
arrived at wisdom I too obtained my reward.

I was innocent of the sin of the Ancient Mariner; time after time I
warned Captain Ahab to accept happiness.

As for Metropolis, that too-great city; her delusions are not mine.

Her speeches impress me little, her statistics less; to all who dwell
on the public side of her mirrors resentments and no peace.

At the place of my passion her photographers are gathered together;
but I shall rise again to hear her judged.

Under Sirius

Yes, these are the dog-days, Fortunatus:
    The heather lies limp and dead
   On the mountain, the baltering torrent
    Shrunk to a soodling thread;
Rusty the spears of the legion, unshaven its captain,
    Vacant the scholar's brain
    Under his great hat,
   Drug as she may the Sibyl utters
    A gush of table-chat.

And you yourself with a head-cold and upset stomach,
    Lying in bed till noon,
   Your bills unpaid, your much advertised
    Epic not yet begun,
Are a sufferer too. All day, you tell us, you wish
    Some earthquake would astonish
    Or the wind of the Comforter's wing
   Unlock the prisons and translate
    The slipshod gathering.

And last night, you say, you dreamed of that bright blue morning,
    The hawthorn hedges in bloom,
   When, serene in their ivory vessels,
    The three wise Maries come,
Sossing through seamless waters, piloted in
    By sea-horse and fluent dolphin:
    Ah! how the cannons roar,
   How jocular the bells as They
    Indulge the peccant shore.

It is natural to hope and pious, of course, to believe
        That all in the end shall be well,
    But first of all, remember,
        So the Sacred Books foretell,
The rotten fruit shall be shaken. Would your hope make sense
        If today were that moment of silence
        Before it break and drown
    When the insurrected eagre hangs
        Over the sleeping town?

How will you look and what will you do when the basalt
        Tombs of the sorcerers shatter
    And their guardian megalopods
        Come after you pitter-patter?
How will you answer when from their qualming spring
        The immortal nymphs fly shrieking
        And out of the open sky
    The pantocratic riddle breaks—
        "Who are you and why?"

For when in a carol under the apple-trees
        The reborn featly dance,
    There will also, Fortunatus,
        Be those who refused their chance,
Now pottering shades, querulous beside the salt-pits,
        And mawkish in their wits,
        To whom these dull dog-days
    Between event seem crowned with olive
        And golden with self-praise.

Not in Baedeker

There were lead-mines here before the Romans,
(Is there a once that is not already?)
Then mines made the manor a looming name
In bridal portions and disputed wills
(Once it changed owners during a card-game),
Then with the coming of the steam-engine
Their heyday arrived (An Early Victorian
Traveller has left us a description:
The removal of the ore, he writes, bless him,
Leaves a horrid gulph. The wild scene is worthy
Of the pencil of Salvator Rosa.
The eye is awe-struck at the extraordinary
Richness of the deposits and the vast
Scale of the operations.), and then, then on
A certain day (whether of time or rock
A lot is only so much and what ends
Ends at a definite moment) there came
Their last day, the day of the last lump, the actual
Day, now vaguely years, say sixty, ago,
When engines and all stopped. Today it would take
A geologist's look to guess that these hills
Provided roofs for some great cathedrals
(One irrevocably damaged by bombs)
And waterproof linings for the coffins
Of statesmen and actresses (all replaced),
Nor could one possibly (because of the odd
Breeding-habits of money, its even
Odder nomadic mania) discover
Where and whom the more than one large fortune
Made here has got to now. A certain place

Has gone back to being (what most of the earth is
Most of the time) in the country somewhere.

Man still however (to discourage any
Romantic glooming over the Universe
Or any one marriage of work and love)
Exists on these uplands and the present
Is not uncheerful: so-so sheep are raised
And sphagnum moss (in the Latin countries
Still used in the treatment of gunshot wounds)
Collected; even the past is not dead
But revives annually on the festival
(Which occurs in the month of the willow)
Of St. Cobalt whose saturnine image,
Crude but certainly medieval is borne
In gay procession around the parish,
Halting at each of the now filled-in shafts
To the shrill chants of little girls in white
And the sneers of the local bus-driver
(Who greases his hair and dreams of halting
For a mysterious well-dressed passenger
Who offers at once to take him to the States).

Indeed, in its own quiet way, the place can strike
Most if not all of the historical notes
Even (what place can not?) the accidental:
One September Thursday two English cyclists
Stopped here for a *fine* and afterwards strolled
Along the no longer polluted stream
As far as the Shot Tower (indirectly
Responsible in its day for the deaths

Of goodness knows how many grouse, wild duck
And magnificent stags) where the younger
(Whose promise one might have guessed even then
Would come to nothing), using a rotting
Rickety gallery for a lectern,
To amuse his friend gave an imitation
Of a clergyman with a cleft palate.

Cattivo Tempo

Sirocco brings the minor devils:
A slamming of doors
At four in the morning
Announces they are back,
Grown insolent and fat
On cheesy literature
And corny dramas,
Nibbar, demon
Of ga-ga and bêtise,
Tubervillus, demon
Of gossip and spite.

Nibbar to the writing-room
Plausibly to whisper
The nearly fine,
The almost true;
Beware of him, poet,
Lest, reading over
Your shoulder, he find
What makes him glad,
The manner arch
The meaning blurred,
The poem bad.

Tubervillus to the dining-room
Intently to listen,
Waiting his cue;
Beware of him, friends,
Lest the talk at his prompting
Take the wrong turning,

The unbated tongue
In mischief blurt
The half-home-truth,
The fun turn ugly,
The jokes hurt.

Do not underrate them; merely
To tear up the poem,
To shut the mouth
Will defeat neither:
To have got you alone
Self-confined to your bedroom
Manufacturing there
From lewdness or self-care
Some whining unmanaged
Imp of your own,
That too is their triumph.

The proper riposte is to bore them;
To scurry the dull pen
Through dull correspondence,
To wag the sharp tongue
In pigeon Italian,
Asking the socialist
Barber to guess
Or the monarchist fishermen to tell
When the wind will change,
Outwitting hell
With human obviousness.

The Chimeras

Absence of heart—as in public buildings,
Absence of mind—as in public speeches,
Absence of worth—as in goods intended for the public,

Are telltale signs that a chimera has just dined
On someone else; of him, poor foolish fellow,
Not a scrap is left, not even his name.

Indescribable—being neither this nor that,
Uncountable—being any number,
Unreal—being anything but what they are,

And ugly customers for someone to encounter,
It is our fault entirely if we do;
They cannot touch us; it is we who will touch them.

Curious from wantonness—to see what they are like,
Cruel from fear—to put a stop to them,
Incredulous from conceit—to prove they cannot be,

We prod or kick or measure and are lost:
The stronger we are the sooner all is over;
It is our strength with which they gobble us up.

If someone, being chaste, brave, humble,
Get by them safely, he is still in danger,
With pity remembering what once they were,

Of turning back to help them. Dont.
What they were once was what they would not be;
Not liking what they are not is what now they are.

No one can help them; walk on, keep on walking,
And do not let your goodness self-deceive you:
It is good that they are but not that they are thus.

Secrets

That we are always glad
When the Ugly Princess parting the bushes
To find out why the woodcutter's children are happy
Disturbs a hornet's nest, that we feel no pity
When the informer is trapped by the gang in a steam-room,
That we howl with joy
When the short-sighted Professor of Icelandic
Pronounces the Greek inscription
A Runic riddle which he then translates,

Denouncing by proxy our commonest fault as our worst;
That, waiting in his room for a friend,
We start so soon to turn over his letters,
That with such assurance we repeat as our own
Another's story, that, dear me, how often
We kiss in order to tell,
Defines precisely what we mean by love:—
To share a secret.

The joke, which we seldom see, is on us;
For only true hearts know how little it matters
What the secret is they keep:
An old, a new, a blue, a borrowed something,
Anything will do for children
Made in God's image and therefore
Not like the others, not like our dear dumb friends
Who, poor things, have nothing to hide,
Not, thank God, like our Father either
From whom no secrets are hid.

Numbers and Faces

The Kingdom of Number is all boundaries
Which may be beautiful and must be true;
To ask if it is big or small proclaims one
The sort of lover who should stick to faces.

Lovers of small numbers go benignly potty,
Believe all tales are thirteen chapters long,
Have animal doubles, carry pentagrams,
Are Millerites, Baconians, Flat-Earth-Men.

Lovers of big numbers go horridly mad,
Would have the Swiss abolished, all of us
Well purged, somatotyped, baptised, taught baseball,
They empty bars, spoil parties, run for Congress.

True, between faces almost any number
Might come in handy, and One is always real;
But which could any face call good, for calling
Infinity a number does not make it one.

Nones

What we know to be not possible
    Though time after time foretold
By wild hermits, by shaman and sybil
    Gibbering in their trances,
Or revealed to a child in some chance rhyme
    Like *will* and *kill*, comes to pass
Before we realise it: we are surprised
    At the ease and speed of our deed
And uneasy: it is barely three,
    Mid afternoon, yet the blood
Of our sacrifice is already
    Dry on the grass; we are not prepared
For silence so sudden and so soon;
    The day is too hot, too bright, too still,
Too ever, the dead remains too nothing.
    What shall we do till nightfall?

The wind has dropped and we have lost our public.
    The faceless many who always
Collect when any world is to be wrecked,
    Blown up, burnt down, cracked open,
Felled, sawn in two, hacked through, torn apart,
    Have all melted away: not one
Of these who in the shade of walls and trees
    Lie sprawled now, calmly sleeping,
Harmless as sheep, can remember why
    He shouted or what about
So loudly in the sunlight this morning;
    All, if challenged, would reply
—"It was a monster with one red eye,

A crowd that saw him die, not I—."
The hangman has gone to wash, the soldiers to eat:
    We are left alone with our feat.

The Madonna with the green woodpecker,
    The Madonna of the fig tree,
The Madonna beside the yellow dam,
    Turn their kind faces from us
And our projects under construction,
    Look only in one direction,
Fix their gaze on our completed work.
    Pile-driver, concrete-mixer,
Crane and pickaxe wait to be used again,
    But how can we repeat this?
Outliving our act we stand where we are
    As disregarded as some
Discarded artifact of our own,
    Like torn gloves, rusted kettles,
Abandoned branchlines, worn lop-sided
    Grindstones buried in nettles.

This mutilated flesh, our victim,
    Explains too nakedly, too well,
The spell of the asparagus garden,
    The aim of our chalk-pit game: stamps,
Bird's eggs are not the same: behind the wonder
    Of tow-paths and sunken lanes,
Behind the rapture on the spiral stair,
    We shall always now be aware
Of the deed into which they lead, under
    The mock chase and mock capture,

The racing and tussling and splashing,
 The panting and the laughter,
Be listening for the cry and stillness
 To follow after. Wherever
The sun shines, brooks run, books are written,
 There will also be this death.

Soon cool tramontana will stir the leaves,
 The shops will re-open at four,
The empty blue bus in the empty pink square
 Fill up and drive off: we have time
To misrepresent, excuse, deny,
 Mythify, use this event
While, under a hotel bed, in prison,
 Down wrong turnings, its meaning
Waits for our lives. Sooner than we would choose
 Bread will melt, water will burn,
And the great quell begin; Abaddon
 Set up his triple gallows
At our seven gates, fat Belial make
 Our wives waltz naked: meanwhile
It would be best to go home, if we have a home,
 In any case good to rest.

That our dreaming wills may seem to escape
 This dead calm, wander instead
On knife edges, on black and white squares,
 Across moss, baize, velvet, boards,
Over cracks and hillocks, in mazes
 Of string and penitent cones,
Down granite ramps and damp passages,

Through gates that will not relatch
And doors marked Private, pursued by Moors
    And watched by latent robbers,
To hostile villages at the heads of fjords,
    To dark châteaux where wind sobs
In the pine-trees and telephones ring
    Inviting trouble, to a room
Lit by one weak bulb where our double sits
    Writing and does not look up.

That while we are thus away our own wronged flesh
    May work undisturbed, restoring
The order we try to destroy, the rhythm
    We spoil out of spite: valves close
And open exactly, glands secrete,
    Vessels contract and expand
At the right moment, essential fluids
    Flow to renew exhausted cells,
Not knowing quite what has happened but awed
    By death like all the creatures
Now watching this spot, like the hawk looking down
    Without blinking, the smug hens
Passing close by in their pecking order,
    The bug whose view is baulked by grass,
Or the deer who shyly from afar
    Peer through chinks in the forest.

A Household

When, to disarm suspicious minds at lunch
Before coming to the point or at golf,
The bargain driven, to soothe hurt feelings,

He talks about his home, he never speaks
(A reticence for which they all admire him)
Of his bride so worshipped and so early lost.

But proudly tells of that young scamp his heir,
Of black eyes given and received, thrashings
Endured without a sound to save a chum;

Or calls their spotted maleness to revere
His saintly mother, calm and kind and wise,
A grand old lady pouring out the tea.

Whom, though, has he ever asked for the week-end?
Out to his country mansion in the evening,
Another merger signed, he drives alone:

To be avoided by a miserable runt
Who wets his bed and cannot throw or whistle,
A tell-tale, a crybaby, a failure;

To the revilings of a slatternly hag
Who caches bottles in her mattress, spits
And shouts obscenities from the landing;

Worse, to find both in an unholy alliance,
Youth stealing Age the liquor-cupboard key,
Age teaching Youth to lie with a straight face.

Disgraces to keep hidden from the world
Where rivals, envying his energy and brains
And with rattling skeletons of their own,

Would see in him the villain of this household,
Whose bull-voice scared a sensitive young child,
Whose coldness drove a doting parent mad.

Besides, (which might explain why he has neither
Altered his will nor called the doctor in)
He half believes, call it a superstition,

It is for his sake that they hate and fear him:
Should they unmask and show themselves worth loving,
Loving and sane and manly, he would die.

The Duet

All winter long the huge sad lady
Sang to her warm house of the heart betrayed:
   Love lies delirious and a-dying,
The purlieus are shaken by his sharp cry.
   But back across the fret dividing
His wildernesses from her floral side
   All winter long a scrunty beggar
With one glass eye and one hickory leg,
   Stumping about half-drunk through stony
Ravines and over dead volcanic cones,
   Refused her tragic hurt, declaring
A happy passion to the freezing air,
   Turning his barrel-organ, playing
Lanterloo, my lovely, my First-of-May.

   Louder on nights when in cold glory
The full moon made its meditative tour,
   To rich chords from her grand black piano
She sang the disappointment and the fear
   For all her lawns and orchards: *Slowly*
The spreading ache bechills the rampant glow
   Of fortune-hunting blood, time conjures
The moskered ancestral tower to plunge
   From its fastidious cornice down to
The pigsties far below, the oaks turn brown,
   The cute little botts of the sailors
Are snapped up by the sea. But to her gale
   Of sorrow from the moonstruck darkness
That ragged runagate opposed his spark,
   For still his scrannel music-making

In tipsy joy across the gliddered lake,
    Praising for all those rocks and craters
The green refreshments of the watered state,
    Cried Nonsense to her large repining:
The windows have opened, a royal wine
    Is poured out for the subtle pudding,
Light Industry is humming in the wood
    And blue birds bless us from the fences,
We know the time and where to find our friends.

Footnotes to Dr. Sheldon

1.

Behold the manly mesomorph
Showing his splendid biceps off,
Whom social workers love to touch,
Though the loveliest girls do not care for him much.

Pretty to watch with bat or ball,
An Achilles, too, in a barroom brawl,
But in the ditch of hopeless odds,
The hour of desertion by brass and gods,

Not a hero. It is the pink-and-white,
Fastidious, slightly girlish, in the night
When the proud-arsed broad-shouldered break and run
Who covers their retreat, dies at his gun.

2.

Give me a doctor partridge-plump,
Short in the leg and broad in the rump,
An endomorph with gentle hands
Who'll never make absurd demands
That I abandon all my vices
Nor pull a long face in a crisis,
But with a twinkle in his eye
Will tell me that I have to die.

Under Which Lyre
A Reactionary Tract for the Times

[PHI BETA KAPPA POEM. HARVARD. 1946]

Ares at last has quit the field,
The bloodstains on the bushes yield
 To seeping showers,
And in their convalescent state
The fractured towns associate
 With summer flowers.

Encamped upon the college plain
Raw veterans already train
 As freshman forces;
Instructors with sarcastic tongue
Shepherd the battle-weary young
 Through basic courses.

Among bewildering appliances
For mastering the arts and sciences
 They stroll or run,
And nerves that never flinched at slaughter
Are shot to pieces by the shorter
 Poems of Donne.

Professors back from secret missions
Resume their proper eruditions,
 Though some regret it;
They liked their dictaphones a lot,
They met some big wheels, and do not
 Let you forget it.

But Zeus' inscrutable decree
Permits the will-to-disagree
        To be pandemic,
Ordains that vaudeville shall preach
And every commencement speech
        Be a polemic.

Let Ares doze, that other war
Is instantly declared once more
        'Twixt those who follow
Precocious Hermes all the way
And those who without qualms obey
        Pompous Apollo.

Brutal like all Olympic games,
Though fought with smiles and Christian names
        And less dramatic,
This dialectic strife between
The civil gods is just as mean,
        And more fanatic.

What high immortals do in mirth
Is life and death on Middle Earth;
        Their a-historic
Antipathy forever gripes
All ages and somatic types,
        The sophomoric

Who face the future's darkest hints
With giggles or with prairie squints
        As stout as Cortez,
And those who like myself turn pale

As we approach with ragged sail
The fattening forties.

The sons of Hermes love to play,
And only do their best when they
Are told they oughtn't;
Apollo's children never shrink
From boring jobs but have to think
Their work important.

Related by antithesis,
A compromise between us is
Impossible;
Respect perhaps but friendship never:
Falstaff the fool confronts forever
The prig Prince Hal.

If he would leave the self alone,
Apollo's welcome to the throne,
Fasces and falcons;
He loves to rule, has always done it;
The earth would soon, did Hermes run it,
Be like the Balkans.

But jealous of our god of dreams,
His common-sense in secret schemes
To rule the heart;
Unable to invent the lyre,
Creates with simulated fire
Official art.

And when he occupies a college,
Truth is replaced by Useful Knowledge;
      He pays particular
Attention to Commercial Thought,
Public Relations, Hygiene, Sport,
      In his curricula

Athletic, extrovert and crude,
For him, to work in solitude
      Is the offence,
The goal a populous Nirvana:
His shield bears this device: *Mens sana*
      Qui mal y pense.

Today his arms, we must confess,
From Right to Left have met success,
      His banners wave
From Yale to Princeton, and the news
From Broadway to the Book Reviews
      Is very grave.

His radio Homers all day long
In over-Whitmanated song
      That does not scan,
With adjectives laid end to end,
Extol the doughnut and commend
      The Common Man.

His, too, each homely lyric thing
On sport or spousal love or spring
      Or dogs or dusters,

Invented by some court-house bard
For recitation by the yard
    In filibusters.

To him ascend the prize orations
And sets of fugal variations
    On some folk-ballad,
While dietitians sacrifice
A glass of prune-juice or a nice
    Marsh-mallow salad.

Charged with his compound of sensational
Sex plus some undenominational
    Religious matter,
Enormous novels by co-eds
Rain down on our defenceless heads
    Till our teeth chatter.

In fake Hermetic uniforms
Behind our battle-line, in swarms
    That keep alighting,
His existentialists declare
That they are in complete despair,
    Yet go on writing.

No matter; He shall be defied;
White Aphrodite is on our side:
    What though his threat
To organize us grow more critical?
Zeus willing, we, the unpolitical,
    Shall beat him yet.

Lone scholars, sniping from the walls
Of learned periodicals,
        Our facts defend,
Our intellectual marines,
Landing in little magazines
        Capture a trend.

By night our student Underground
At cocktail parties whisper round
        From ear to ear;
Fat figures in the public eye
Collapse next morning, ambushed by
        Some witty sneer.

In our morale must lie our strength:
So, that we may behold at length
        Routed Apollo's
Battalions melt away like fog,
Keep well the Hermetic Decalogue,
        Which runs as follows:—

Thou shalt not do as the dean pleases,
Thou shalt not write thy doctor's thesis
        On education,
Thou shalt not worship projects nor
Shalt thou or thine bow down before
        Administration.

Thou shalt not answer questionnaires
Or quizzes upon World-Affairs,
        Nor with compliance

Take any test. Thou shalt not sit
With statisticians nor commit
　　　A social science.

Thou shalt not be on friendly terms
With guys in advertising firms,
　　　Nor speak with such
As read the Bible for its prose,
Nor, above all, make love to those
　　　Who wash too much.

Thou shalt not live within thy means
Nor on plain water and raw greens.
　　　If thou must choose
Between the chances, choose the odd;
Read *The New Yorker*, trust in God;
　　　And take short views.

To
T. S. Eliot
On His Sixtieth Birthday

[1948]

When things began to happen to our favorite spot,
A key missing, a library bust defaced,
    Then on the tennis-court one morning,
    Outrageous, the bloody corpse and always,

Blank day after day, the unheard-of drought, it was you
Who, not speechless from shock but finding the right
    Language for thirst and fear, did much to
    Prevent a panic. It is the crime that

Counts, you will say. We know, but would gratefully add,
Today as we wait for the Law to take its course,
    (And which of us shall escape whipping?)
    That your sixty years have not been wasted.

Music Is International

[PHI BETA KAPPA POEM. COLUMBIA. 1947]

Orchestras have so long been speaking
This universal language that the Greek
    And the Barbarian have both mastered
Its enigmatic grammar which at last
    Says all things well. But who is worthy?
What is sweet? What is sound? Much of the earth
    Is austere, her temperate regions
Swarming with cops and robbers; germs besiege
    The walled towns and among the living
The captured outnumber the fugitive.
    Where silence is coldest and darkest,
Among those staring blemishes that mark
    War's havocking slot, it is easy
To guess what dreams such vaulting cries release:
    The unamerican survivor
Hears angels drinking fruit-juice with their wives
    Or making money in an open
Unpolicied air. But what is our hope
    As with an ostentatious rightness
These gratuitous sounds like water and light
    Bless the Republic? Do they sponsor
In us the mornes and motted mammelons,
    The sharp streams and sottering springs of
A commuter's wish, where each frescade rings
    With melodious booing and hooing
As some elegant lovejoy deigns to woo
    And nothing dreadful ever happened?
Probably yes. We are easy to trap,
    Being Adam's children, as thirsty

For mere illusion still as when the first
    Comfortable heresy crooned to
The proud flesh founded on the self-made wound,
    And what we find rousing or touching
Tells us little and confuses us much.
    As Shaw says—Music is the brandy
Of the damned. It was from the good old grand
    Composers the progressive kind of
Tyrant learned how to melt the legal mind
    With a visceral A-ha; fill a
Dwarf's ears with sforzandos and the dwarf will
    Believe he's a giant; the orchestral
Metaphor bamboozles the most oppressed
    —As a trombone the clerk will bravely
Go oompah-oompah to his minor grave—
    So that today one recognises
The Machiavel by the hair in his eyes,
    His conductor's hands. Yet the jussive
Elohim are here too, asking for us
    Through the noise. To forgive is not so
Simple as it is made to sound; a lot
    Of time will be quite wasted, many
Promising days end badly and again
    We shall offend: but let us listen
To the song which seems to absorb all this,
    For these halcyon structures are useful
As structures go—though not to be confused
    With anything really important
Like feeding strays or looking pleased when caught
    By a bore or a hideola;
Deserving nothing, the sensible soul

73

Will rejoice at the sudden mansion
Of any joy; besides, there is a chance
    We may some day need very much to
Remember when we were happy—one such
    Future would be the exile's ending
With no graves to visit, no socks to mend,
    Another to be short of breath yet
Staying on to oblige, postponing death—
    Listen! Even the dinner waltz in
Its formal way is a voice that assaults
    International wrong, so quickly,
Completely delivering to the sick,
    Sad, soiled prosopon of our ageing
Present the perdition of all her rage.

Precious Five

Be patient, solemn nose,
Serve in a world of prose
The present moment well
Nor surlily contrast
Its brash ill-mannered smell
With grand scents of the past;
That calm enchanted wood,
That grave world where you stood
So gravely at its middle,
Its oracle and riddle,
Has all been altered, now
In anxious times you serve
As bridge from mouth to brow,
As asymmetric curve
Thrust outward from a face
Time-conscious into space,
Whose oddness may provoke
To a mind-saving joke
A mind that would it were
An apathetic sphere:
Point, then, for honor's sake
Up the storm-beaten slope
From memory to hope
The way you cannot take.

Be modest, lively ears,
Spoiled darlings of a stage
Where any caper cheers
The paranoic mind
Of this undisciplined

And concert-going age,
So lacking in conviction
It cannot take pure fiction
And what it wants from you
Are rumors partly true;
Before you catch its sickness
Submit your lucky quickness
And levity to rule,
Go back again to school,
Drudge patiently until
No whisper is too much
And your precision such
At any sound that all
Seem natural, not one
Fantastic or banal,
And then do what you will:
Dance with angelic grace,
In ecstasy and fun,
The luck you cannot place.

Be civil, hands; on you
Although you cannot read
Is written what you do
And blows you struck so blindly
In temper or in greed,
Your tricks of long ago,
Eyes, kindly or unkindly,
Unknown to you will know;
Revere those hairy wrists
And leg-of-mutton fists
Which pulverised the trolls

And carved deep Donts in stone,
Great hands which under knolls
Are now disjointed bone,
But what has been has been;
A tight arthritic claw
Or aldermanic paw
Waving about in praise
Of those homeric days
Is impious and obscene:
Grow, hands, into those living
Hands which true hands should be
By making and by giving
To hands you cannot see.

Look, naked eyes, look straight
At all eyes but your own
Lest in a tête-à-tête
Of glances double-crossed,
Both knowing and both known,
Your nakedness be lost;
Rove curiously about
But look from inside out,
Compare two eyes you meet
By dozens on the street,
One shameless, one ashamed,
Too lifeless to be blamed,
With eyes met now and then
Looking from living men,
Which in petrarchan fashion
Play opposite the heart,
Their humor to her passion,

Her nature to their art,
For mutual undeceiving;
True seeing is believing
(What sight can never prove)
There is a world to see:
Look outward, eyes, and love
Those eyes you cannot be.

Praise, tongue, the Earthly Muse
By number and by name
In any style you choose,
For nimble tongues and lame
Have both found favor; praise
Her port and sudden ways,
Now fish-wife and now queen,
Her reason and unreason:
Though freed from that machine,
Praise Her revolving wheel
Of appetite and season
In honor of Another,
The old self you become
At any drink or meal,
That animal of taste
And of his twin, your brother,
Unlettered, savage, dumb,
Down there below the waist:
Although your style be fumbling,
Half stutter and half song,
Give thanks however bumbling,
Telling for Her dear sake

To whom all styles belong
The truth She cannot make.

Be happy, precious five,
So long as I'm alive
Nor try to ask me what
You should be happy for;
Think, if it helps, of love
Or alcohol or gold,
But do as you are told.
I could (which you cannot)
Find reasons fast enough
To face the sky and roar
In anger and despair
At what is going on,
Demanding that it name
Whoever is to blame:
The sky would only wait
Till all my breath was gone
And then reiterate
As if I wasn't there
That singular command
I do not understand,
Bless what there is for being,
Which has to be obeyed, for
What else am I made for,
Agreeing or disagreeing.

A Walk After Dark

A cloudless night like this
Can set the spirit soaring;
After a tiring day
The clockwork spectacle is
Impressive in a slightly boring
Eighteenth-century way.

It soothed adolescence a lot
To meet so shameless a stare;
The things I did could not
Be as shocking as they said
If that would still be there
After the shocked were dead.

Now, unready to die
But already at the stage
When one starts to dislike the young,
I am glad those points in the sky
May also be counted among
The creatures of middle-age.

It's cosier thinking of night
As more an Old People's Home
Than a shed for a faultless machine,
That the red pre-Cambrian light
Is gone like Imperial Rome
Or myself at seventeen.

Yet however much we may like
The stoic manner in which

The classical authors wrote,
Only the young and the rich
Have the nerve or the figure to strike
The lacrimae rerum note.

For the present stalks abroad
Like the past and its wronged again
Whimper and are ignored,
And the truth cannot be hid;
Somebody chose their pain,
What needn't have happened did.

Occurring this very night
By no established rule,
Some event may already have hurled
Its first little No at the right
Of the laws we accept to school
Our post-diluvian world:

But the stars burn on overhead,
Unconscious of final ends,
As I walk home to bed,
Asking what judgment waits
My person, all my friends,
And these United States.